Quiet as a Butterfly

I Wonder Why

Quiet as a Butterfly

By Lawrence F. Lowery

Illustrated by Ati Forberg

NSTA Kids
National Science Teachers Association
Arlington, Virginia

One day, I listened.
I listened to all the sounds I heard.
I listened, and I wondered.

I can hear the
clock ticking,
birds singing,
roosters crowing,
dogs barking.

Yellow butterfly,
I wonder why
I can't hear you.

I can hear the
milk bottles banging,
doors slamming,
a big clock chiming,
a baby crying.

Golden flower,
I wonder why
I can't hear you.

I can hear
Mother humming,
dishes clinking,
bacon sizzling,
Father whistling.

Little ladybug,
I wonder why
I can't hear you.

I can hear
ladies talking,
chickens clucking,
cat meowing,
bumblebee buzzing.

Funny spider,
I wonder why
I can't hear you.

I can hear horns beeping,
whistles blowing,
sirens screaming,
engines roaring.

Puffy cloud,
I wonder why
I can't hear you.

I can hear the
school bell ringing,
teacher reading,
girls laughing,
boys giggling.

Shiny goldfish,
I wonder why
I can't hear you.

I can hear
flutes tweeting,
trumpets blaring,
drums booming,
cymbals clashing.

Tiny ant,
I wonder why
I can't hear you.

I can hear
leaves rustling,
wind whistling,
thunder clapping,
rain dripping.

Wiggly worm,
I wonder why
I can't hear you.

I can hear
crows cawing,
children shouting,
pigeons fluttering,
frogs croaking.

Slippery snail,
I wonder why
I can't hear you.

I can hear
Mother singing,
Father laughing,
pots banging,
pans clanging.

Fuzzy caterpillar,
I wonder why
I can't hear you.

I can hear
needles clicking,
kitten purring,
chair rocking,
Father snoring.

Sleepy turtle,
I wonder why
I can't hear you.

I can hear the
staircase creaking,
far trains tooting,
wise owl ... hooting,
clock ... tick ... ing.

Firefly, I wonder why ...

And the boy fell asleep
thinking of all the sounds
he heard that day.
Some sounds were loud.
Some sounds were soft,
some sweet, some low, some high.

Some things he only saw.
And they were
as quiet as a butterfly.

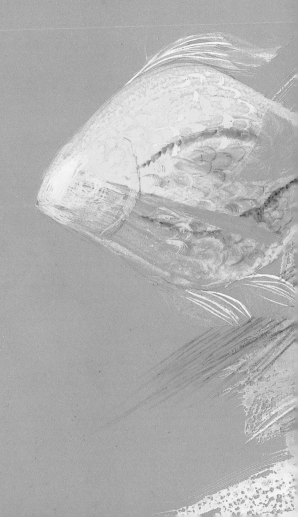

Quiet as a Butterfly

Parent/Teacher Handbook

Introduction

Our everyday life includes many sounds. Even if our hearing is good, many of these sounds we do not hear—but we could if we would only listen. This is a listening book. In it, a young boy "listens" his way through a school day. He realizes he can hear more sounds if he listens closely, but some sounds cannot be heard because of their intensity or pitch.

Inquiry Processes

Quiet as a Butterfly stresses listening as an observational skill. The sounds that the young boy hears pertain to particular places or times of day. The reader should sense, through visual and contextual clues, the flow of time through the boy's day, even though time is never explicit in the story.

Nearly every page of this book introduces organisms. Many organisms produce sounds, but some make sounds that our ears cannot hear. The statement "I wonder why I can't hear you" invites readers to think about sounds that are too soft or too high for their ears to detect.

Content

Next to our sense of sight, hearing is probably our most useful sense. We communicate by talking to each other, and we have invented instruments that enable us to hear sounds we cannot normally hear. The physician uses a stethoscope to bring information to her ears that her eyes cannot see. Hearing aids enable people who are hard of hearing to hear better. Scientists often use listening devices to gather sounds from outer space or from the depths of the oceans. Hearing and technological extensions of hearing (e.g., sonar) give us knowledge of happenings at a distance.

On Earth, vibrations of matter such as air, water, or a solid material create sound. No sound occurs in a vacuum. When a person speaks, the vocal cords vibrate, causing the air passing out of the lungs to vibrate. The vibrations are bands of compressed air followed by bands of less compressed air. The vibrations are somewhat like ripples on the surface of water.

Volume, which we use to describe how loud a sound is, is a function of wave height. The higher the wave, the louder the sound. **Pitch**, which we use to describe high and low sounds, is a function of the wave frequency (the number of waves per second). The greater the frequency, the higher the sound.

The shape of our ears helps collect sounds and direct them into our auditory canal. Our auditory system then enables us to identify and recognize sounds, words, and music.

Our sense of hearing cannot be shut off as our sense of sight can when we close our eyes. Sounds enter our ears at all times, even when we are asleep. Our brain, however, can dim out sounds around us so that we can focus our attention on sounds we choose to hear.

This book provides a descriptive focus on the many sounds and sound-makers in a child's world and stresses the importance of attending to and differentiating sounds.

Science Activities

Identifying Patterns in Sounds

Play a tapping game with the reader. Tap evenly several times on a table or desk. Ask how many taps were heard, or have the reader repeat the number of taps. With practice, the reader can reproduce different rhythms and changes between loud and soft.

Listening to Verbal Directions

To improve the reader's ability to listen carefully, play Simon Says. Pretend you are Simon and tell the reader what he or she must do. The reader must only obey commands that begin with the words "Simon says." If you say, "Simon says touch your nose," then the reader must touch his or her nose. But if you say only, "Touch your nose," the reader must not touch his or her nose. Stress the importance of listening carefully to follow directions.

Listening to Verbal Information

In a room with five or more people, tell the reader you will describe someone in the room. Describe the person gradually. For example, say, "I am thinking of a person with brown hair ... blue eyes ... who is a girl ... who is wearing a white dress ..." As soon as the reader recognizes who the person is from the verbal descriptions, he or she should say, "I have enough information." Then, the reader can identify the person.

Locating the Source of Sounds

The place where a sound originates is sometimes difficult to determine. Our ability to locate such places improves with practice.

Have the reader sit near the center of a room. Blindfold the reader and stand in front of him or her and demonstrate the sound you will make. The sound might simply be a snap of your fingers or a one-tone sound-maker. Have the reader look straight ahead while you move around the room and make the sound. The reader then points to the direction

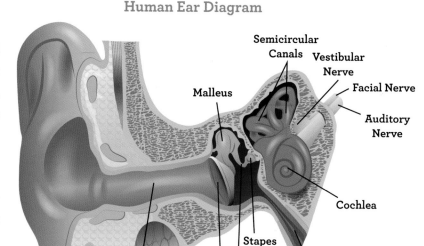

Human Ear Diagram

Semicircular Canals
Vestibular Nerve
Facial Nerve
Malleus
Auditory Nerve
Cochlea
Stapes
Eustachian Tube
Incus
Ear Canal
Eardrum

from which the sound comes. Note where the reader points, and keep a record of where the sound is most difficult to hear. Sometimes make the sound below or above the reader's head. With practice, the reader's ability to locate sounds will improve.

Vary the activity by playing music in the background. The music will require the reader to concentrate more intently on the sound you make. You can also change the activity by having the reader press one ear closed while he or she tries to locate sounds. Then, make the sounds again from the same locations when the reader has both ears open. Compare the differences in the reader's ability to locate the sounds. Do the same with the reader's other ear closed.

Identifying Objects That Make Sounds

Make a recording of sounds from home (e.g., whistling tea kettle, washing machine or dryer, vacuum cleaner, ticking clock, ringing alarm clock, egg beater). Have the reader describe the sounds and identify the various objects that make the sounds.